Ellie,
We hope
you come to many
visit Arizona
time?
Jan &
Hermann
November 2015

ZONA 1912

MARSHALL EXPLORES ARIZONA

By ANGELA and WILLIAM KIRSCHNER

Designed & Illustrated by Mike Miller

An Exploring Eagle Press Publication

www.exploringeaglepress.com

In memory of Arthur Evans, my Granddad, who inspired me to write poetry at a young age and taught me the importance of integrity and perseverance. AK

A special thank-you to our parents for your unwavering love and support. You've shaped who we are today. AK & WK

Composed in the United States of America   Printed in China, Job #A-18
Edited by Karen Schader   Illustrated by Mike Miller

First Edition. Published in April 2010.

Publisher's Cataloging-in-Publication

    Kirschner, Angela.
      Marshall explores Arizona / by Angela Kirschner &
    William Kirschner ; illustrated by Mike Miller. -- 1st
    ed.
      p. cm.
      SUMMARY: Marshall, a bald eagle, explores the state
    of Arizona, visiting historical and notable places, like
    the Grand Canyon. Marshall teaches the reader about
    Arizona plants, animals, and geography. This fully
    illustrated book has both a rhyming section for young
    children and a more factual prose part for older kids.
      Audience: Ages 1-12.
      LCCN 2009942331
      ISBN-13: 978-0-9825845-0-7
      ISBN-10: 0-9825845-0-4

      1. Arizona--Description and travel--Juvenile
    literature. [1. Arizona--Description and travel.]
    I. Kirschner, William. II. Miller, Mike (Michael D.), ill.
    III. Title.

    F815.K57 2010   917'.910454
                      QBI09-600222

For our Ethan:
Life is an adventure.
Enjoy every step of your journey
And continue to smell the flowers.
With much love,
AK & WK

Hi! I'm Marshall, the Eagle, off to explore Arizona. Come join me! On our trip, we'll visit places high up in the snow-capped mountains and way down in the desert. We'll see Native American ruins, a desert that looks painted, the Grand Canyon, and more. Keep an eye out for sneaky coyotes and zippy roadrunners, and make sure to stay away from the prickly cacti. Also look for the cactus wren, Arizona's state bird, on every page. Let's go explore!

Welcome to Arizona, the Grand Canyon State,
Where mountains, deserts, and coyotes await.
There are cacti, snakes, and scorpions galore,
And beautiful sunsets that many adore.

Arizona is such an interesting state—
Let's go explore; it will be great!

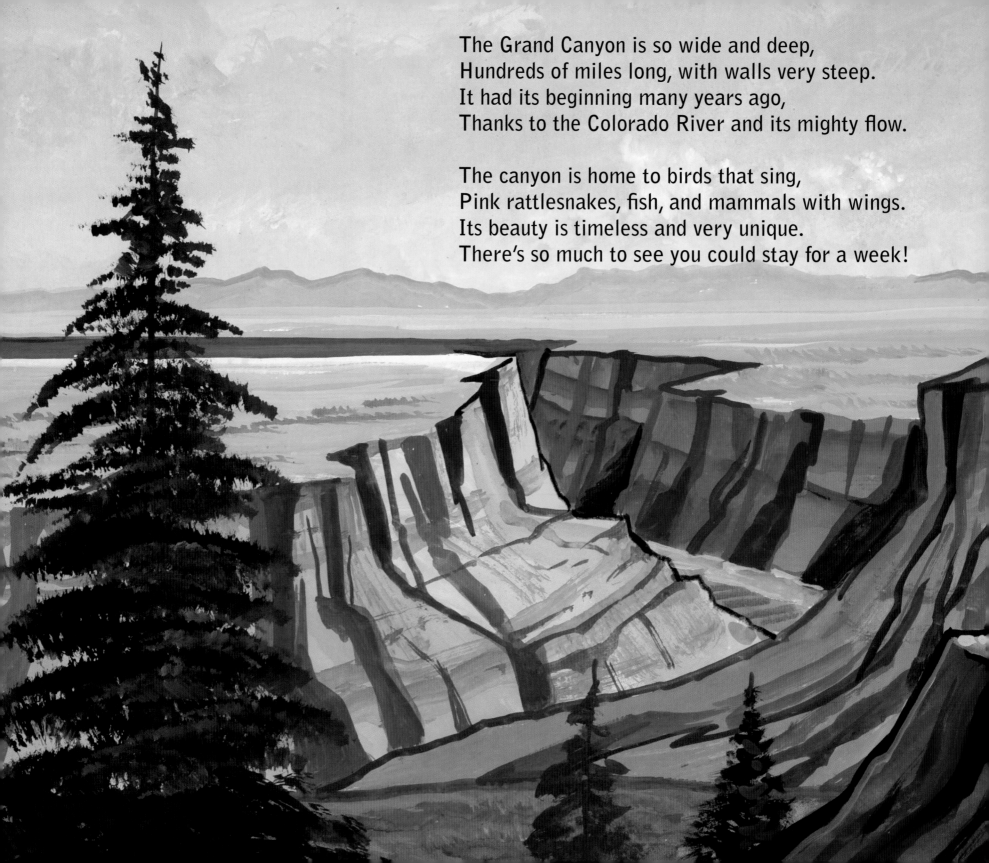

The Grand Canyon is so wide and deep,
Hundreds of miles long, with walls very steep.
It had its beginning many years ago,
Thanks to the Colorado River and its mighty flow.

The canyon is home to birds that sing,
Pink rattlesnakes, fish, and mammals with wings.
Its beauty is timeless and very unique.
There's so much to see you could stay for a week!

Can you guess how long the Grand Canyon is?

I'll tell you—277 miles! At its widest point, it is 15 miles across, and in some spots, it is more than a mile deep. The canyon was carved out over many, many years through erosion, as the Colorado River ate away at the surrounding stone. In 1908, President Theodore Roosevelt named the Grand Canyon a national monument. It became a national park in 1919.

While we're there, we may see squirrels, mule deer, elk, mountain lions, bats, and even bald eagles like me! We'll see lots of people, too. Nearly 5 million of them visit the Grand Canyon every year.

There's a spot you can stand in four states at one time.
You can visit the Painted Desert, with colors so fine.

The Petrified Forest is not full of trees,
But there are rocks and fossils for you to see.

COLORADO

UTAH

NEW
MEXICO

ARIZONA

In northeastern Arizona, we'll find some fascinating geological formations. The Painted Desert looks like someone took a brush and painted the rocks and hills in a rainbow of colors. Nearby is the Petrified Forest National Park, but it isn't like a regular forest. Everything there is as hard as a rock; in fact, everything there is a rock!

Thousands of years ago, North American Indians lived in this "forest." It became a national monument in 1906. Let's keep an eye out for fossils, too, which can be found just lying on the ground.

While we're visiting the Painted Desert and Petrified Forest, we can make a trip to Four Corners, the only place in the United States where four states meet. If you stand just right, you can be in Colorado, Arizona, New Mexico, and Utah— all at the same time!

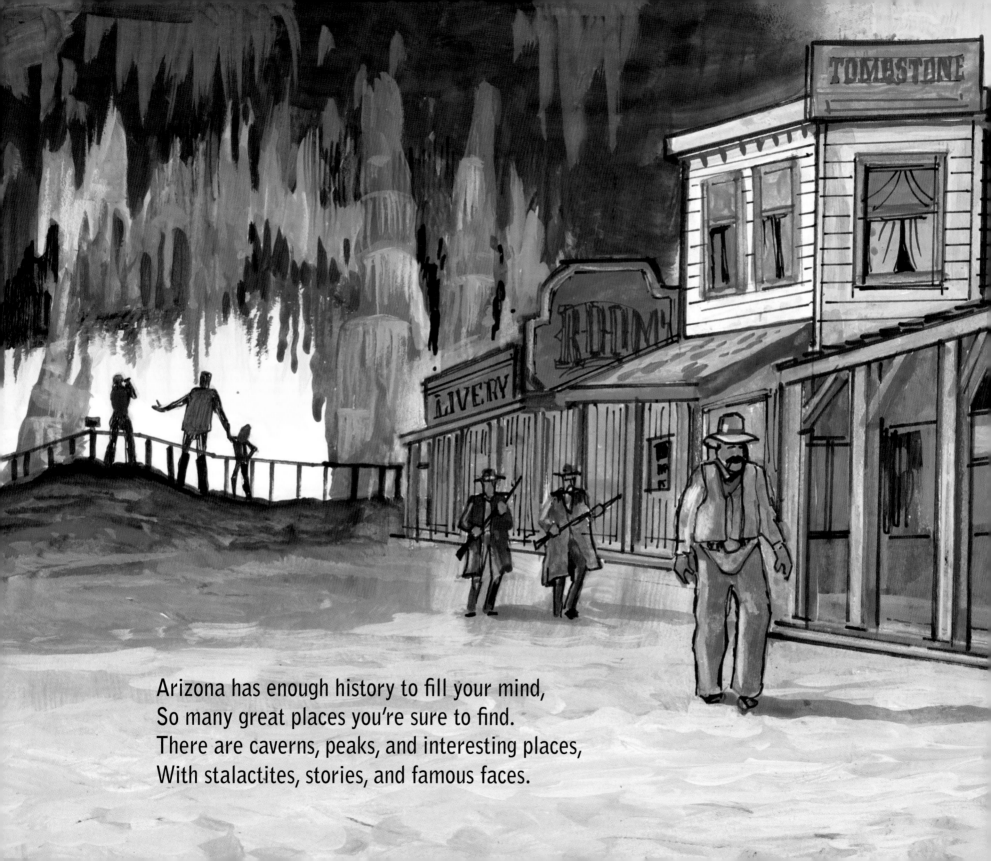

Arizona has enough history to fill your mind,
So many great places you're sure to find.
There are caverns, peaks, and interesting places,
With stalactites, stories, and famous faces.

Okay, we're off to southern Arizona now.

One of this area's many fascinating spots is Kartchner Caverns State Park. Its cave, with stalactites (stone formations that grow down from the cave's ceiling) and stalagmites (which grow up from its floor), was discovered in 1974. It was kept secret for many years because the owners were concerned about visitors destroying its natural beauty. But today we can take a guided tour and see this amazing underground world for ourselves.

Did you ever hear of Tombstone? It's the home of the O.K. Corral, where a world-famous shoot-out took place in 1881. Today, Tombstone is a small town, but back in the time of the shoot-out, it was as large as the city of Tucson. And did you know that the Civil War reached as far as Arizona? A mountain called Picacho Peak was the site of a Civil War battle in 1862. Every March, the battle is reenacted at Picacho Peak State Park.

The Hoover Dam is really tall
With tons of concrete in its walls.

The water on one side forms Lake Mead,
A lake that is huge and deep, indeed!

The London Bridge that was falling down
Was moved years ago to an Arizona town.
Lake Havasu City is where it resides,
A place for fun and summer boat rides.

Imagine a road that runs from San Francisco to New York City.

Well, the Hoover Dam contains enough concrete to pave that road! It is more than 726 feet high, and it took 21,000 men seven years to build. When the dam was built, water from the Colorado River (the same river that flows through the Grand Canyon) backed up behind it. That water formed a huge lake, known as Lake Mead.

Two hours south of the Hoover Dam, we come to the London Bridge. Yes, the London Bridge—the one in the song—really was falling down. But instead of fixing it, the British government decided to sell it. The bridge was moved to Lake Havasu City and reopened to traffic in 1971.

Believe it or not, people ski here as well.
Northern Arizona is where the snow dwells.
Above the Mogollon Rim, where it gets quite cold,
There's even a volcano that's centuries old.

It's time to cool off!

With its tall pine trees and mountains, northern Arizona is much cooler than the lower half of the state. One of the many beautiful places to see is Sedona. Its limestone hills, deposited there many, many years ago by a shallow tropical sea, are rusty red because of the iron in the rocks. The town was originally called Indian Gardens but was renamed Sedona in 1902.

Flagstaff is home to Northern Arizona University. About one mile above sea level, Flagstaff has great winter skiing and is also home to Sunset Crater Volcano National Monument. But don't worry, this dormant volcano hasn't erupted in over a thousand years.

A very, very long time ago,
Native Americans traveled through desert and snow.
They farmed and worked long days in the heat.
Surviving here was no small feat!

Apache and Mohave were two of the tribes.
The Sinaguas built a dwelling high in the sky.
Montezuma Castle is its name;
While the tribe disappeared, the castle remains.

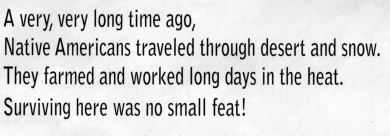

Native Americans

played an important role in Arizona's history, and the oldest tribe can trace its roots back two thousand years. Montezuma Castle, near Sedona, is a twenty-room "house" built into the side of a cliff. What happened to the Sinagua Indians who lived there hundreds of years ago is still a mystery. What do you think?

Today, the federal government recognizes twenty-one tribes in Arizona. With over 250,000 members, these tribes are an important part of the state's population. Their culture lives on in many ways: pottery, jewelry, music, and dance, to name a few.

Arizona's a great place to go to college.
Wherever you go, you'll gain much knowledge.
ASU, U of A, and NAU—
Which one of these sounds good to you?

Lots of high school graduates head to Arizona every year.

The three largest schools are Arizona State University, the University of Arizona, and Northern Arizona University. Together, these schools have more than 100,000 full-time students. Arizona State is in Tempe, just outside of Phoenix in central Arizona, and its sports teams are known as the Sun Devils. The University of Arizona Wildcats are in Tucson, in the southern part of the state. And the Northern Arizona Lumberjacks are up north in Flagstaff, where you'll find Humphrey's Peak, the highest point in Arizona at over 12,000 feet.

When you're ready to think about college, keep the Grand Canyon State in mind!

ASU

In March people go to spring training games.
The Suns are the best, at least that's what some claim.
There are also Cardinals, Coyotes, and Diamondbacks.
The sports teams are talented, and that's a fact.

If you're a basketball fan, you've probably heard of Charles Barkley, Dan Majerle, Shaquille O'Neal, and Steve Nash. They are some of the most famous stars who have played for the Phoenix Suns, Arizona's professional basketball team.

Arizona has other pro teams, too. The Diamondbacks won the baseball World Series in 2001; and the Cardinals, one of the original pro football teams, have played in Arizona since 1988. And hot as Arizona can be, it still has a hockey team: the Coyotes. Arizona is also home to the Cactus League, a baseball spring training league that plays in the month of March and has been around for more than fifty years.

The desert is hot and also dry,
One hundred degrees is often the high!
Believe it or not, it can rain here,
And when it does everyone cheers!
The rain comes down so fast and hard
That children go out and run in the yard.

Much of Arizona is located in the Sonoran Desert, which is the hottest desert in the United States. Fierce dust storms, called haboobs, sometimes blow through the Sonoran Desert. There's only one other place in the world where haboobs happen: the Sahara Desert in Northern Africa.

Arizona receives most of its rain in the summer, during storms that are known as monsoon thunderstorms. Monsoon thunderstorms occur when swirling winds pick up moisture from the Pacific Ocean and the Gulf of Mexico. They can bring damaging winds, hail, and very heavy rain.

There are lots of cacti to look at and admire,
And sometimes lightning strikes set them on fire.
They all store water and some have fruit,
But make sure not to touch them—they're spiky to boot!

There are many animals that roam about—
Can you believe they survive the droughts?
Like javelina, bobcats, and rattlesnakes
Plus ducks and fish that swim in the lakes.

One of four deserts in North America, the Sonoran Desert has temperatures that can top one hundred ten degrees in the summer. Its most famous plant is probably the saguaro (sah-wah-roh) cactus. This type of cactus grows only one to two inches a year, which means that many of the saguaros we'll see are over a hundred years old!

Many different animals live in this Arizona desert, including javelina (hav-a-leen-a), coyotes, jackrabbits, rattlesnakes, and roadrunners. Javelina look a lot like wild pigs, but they are not pigs; they are actually members of the peccary family. If we're out in the desert at night, we might even hear javelina scavenging for food.

Arizona is abbreviated with an A and a Z,
The start and end of the alphabet—that's so easy to me!
In 1912, Arizona became a state,
On Valentine's Day, a memorable date.

Arizona's history

dates back thousands of years, but it is one of the youngest states in the United States. Arizona became the forty-eighth state in 1912, followed only by Alaska and Hawaii. Before that, Arizona was considered a territory and did not have a governor and legislators like states do today. Arizona's capitol is now located in Phoenix.

There are different ideas about where the state's name came from, and no one knows for sure. One possibility is that it was named after a ranch called Arizona, which means "the good oak tree" in Basque. Basque was the language of many of the original settlers who lived near the ranch. I bet you can guess what kind of trees grew nearby!

Five Cs helped Arizona grow
Into the great place we now know.
Copper and cattle and cotton too,
Plus citrus and climate—and a sky so blue!

Arizona is still known for its copper today,
And the climate is welcoming in the winter, I'd say.
While pima cotton blows in the breeze,
You can grab a sweet orange off a citrus tree.

Five Cs—copper, cattle, cotton, citrus, and climate—helped to shape and grow the state of Arizona.

By 1863, about one out of every four people were miners. In fact, copper is still mined in Arizona. In 1918, cattle ranches covered the state, and ranching continues to be a big part of Arizona's culture. Many farmers in the early 1900s grew a kind of cotton known as pima, and Arizona today is one of the leading cotton-producing states in the United States. Do you like oranges? You can find citrus farms throughout Arizona, and many people have citrus trees in their yards. The fifth C is for climate: lots of visitors come to Arizona year-round, but particularly in the winter months when they leave the colder northern states behind.

Goodbye from Arizona

I hope you enjoyed our trip together.
Were you surprised by Arizona's hot weather?
Now get ready, get set, and off we go—
We have many more states to explore, you know!

Thanks for traveling through Arizona with me!

I hope you enjoyed the adventure and have the chance to visit these places in person someday.

Join me, Marshall the Eagle, when I visit another state; I look forward to our next exploration together!

ARIZONA

State Bird: Cactus Wren

State Tree: Palo Verde

State Fossil: Petrified Wood

State Gemstone: Turquoise

State Fish: Apache Trout

State Mammal: Ringtail

State Flower: Saguaro Cactus Blossom

State Flag: The Arizona flag was designed by Colonel Charles W. Harris and was officially adopted in 1917. The red and yellow rays represent the sunshine and the original 13 colonies. Those were also the colors of the Spanish Conquistadors flag that entered the territory in 1540. The copper star represents copper mining, a major Arizona natural resource.

Nickname: Grand Canyon State

Admitted to Statehood: February 14, 1912

Square Miles: 113,909
State Colors: Blue, Old Gold

State Song: Arizona March Song

Largest Cities: Phoenix, Tucson, Mesa, Glendale, Scottsdale, Chandler, Tempe, Gilbert, Peoria, Yuma

Major Rivers: Colorado, Salt, Verde, Gila

Major Lakes: Mead, Powell, Roosevelt, Lake Pleasant, Saguaro, Canyon, San Carlos, Mojave

Highest Point: Humphries Peak, Flagstaff

For Census and Demographics:
http://quickfacts.census.gov

Where is Arizona?